# HE WHO LISTENS

AN INUIT STORY
FROM ALASKA

Once upon a time, an old man
was out on the ice hunting seals.
He crouched in the cold air, listening, listening,
for the sounds that would tell him
that the seals were coming up their breathing holes
in the ice.

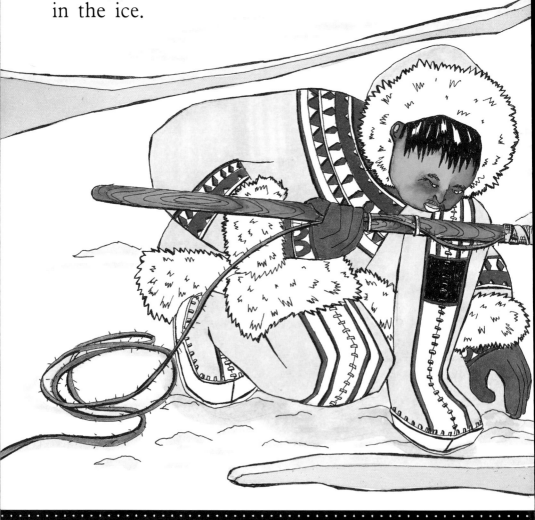

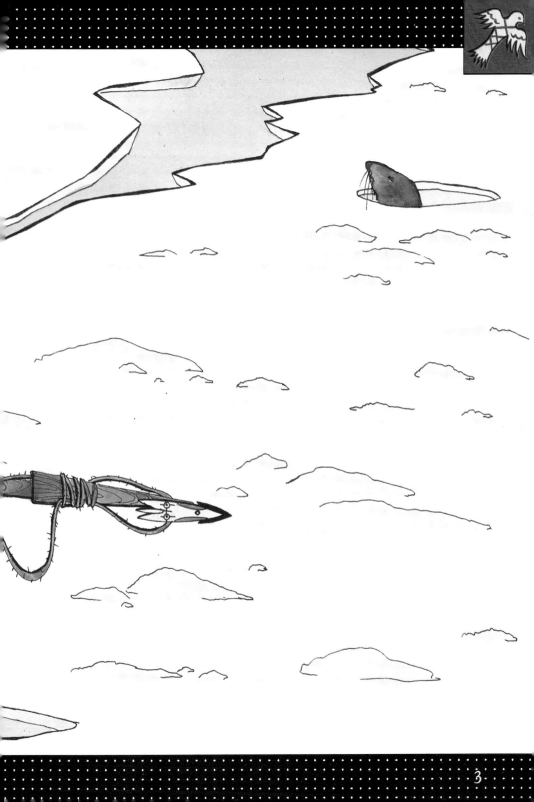

As he waited motionless,
some children ran near him,
and their laughter and noise
scared the seals away.

The old man was very angry,
and he shouted at the children.
His shouting caused an ice cliff
to fall on the children.

As the cliff crashed down,
only one boy escaped.

The boy ran home and told his father and mother what had happened.
They called the other people in the village, and, together, they all ran out to the ice.

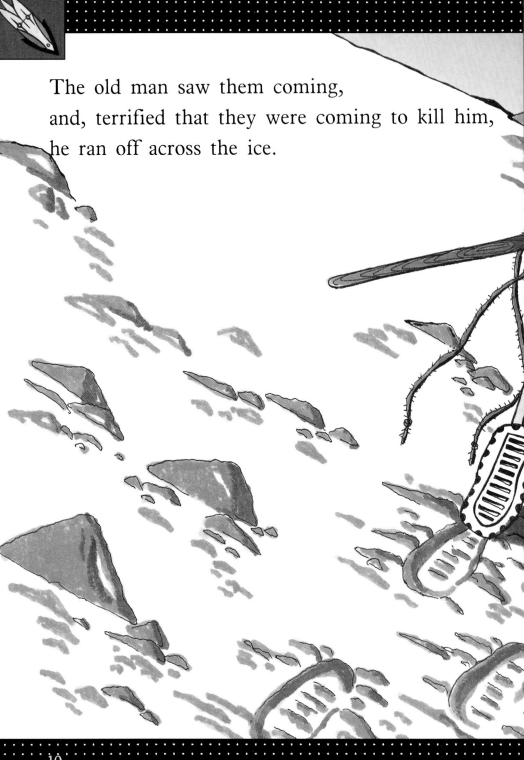

The old man saw them coming,
and, terrified that they were coming to kill him,
he ran off across the ice.

Faster and faster he ran,
until he was running so fast
that his feet began to climb into the sky.

Up there,
he turned into the star we call Venus.

Venus always appears to be low in the sky.
The Inuit say
that it is really the old man,
listening for the sound of the seals
coming up at their breathing holes.

We often call Venus
the morning or evening star,
but the Inuit name for it is
*He Who Listens.*